contents

60p

11/2

NZ, Canada, US and UK readers
Please note that Australian cup and spoon
measurements are metric. A quick conversion
guide appears on page 63.

Cheers!

Store-bought drinks and juices are convenient, but take a little time to prepare a drink at home and it will leave the store-made version for dead. The recipes in this book will walk you through juice combinations, smoothies, lassis and frappés to kickstart your day, iced drinks to quench a summer thirst, punches that will really get the party started, and some hot and spicy drinks to help you nod off in front of a glowing fire in winter.

equipment

Most of the drinks in this book are made using either a blender or a juice extractor. Juices and smoothies prepared in a blender contain a good dose of fibre as the fruit/vegetable pulp is mixed through the drink; drinks prepared in a juice extractor, however, contain only the juice.

Blenders are best suited to soft fruits, such as mangoes, stone fruit, bananas and berries, especially when milk, yogurt or crushed ice is being added. Basically, they are ideal for the preparation of smoothies, lassis and frappés.

Juice extractors are ideal for use with hard fruit and vegetables such as apples, citrus, carrot, celery and other leafy greens.

An important consideration when purchasing a blender or juice extractor is how easy it is to keep clean. Any appliance you use for juicing and/or blending should be cleaned immediately, otherwise the fruit pulp can prove very difficult to remove.

drinks by definition

smoothie

A smoothie is a combination of fruit and dairy products, such as milk, ice-cream or yogurt, that is blended until thick and smooth.

frappé

A frappé is a frozen flavoured liquid (usually a blend of whole fruit – mangoes, pineapple, etc – or fruit juice with crushed ice) that has a slushy consistency.

lassi

A lassi is an Indian version of a milkshake, except that yogurt is used in place of milk. A variety of spices and fruits can be added to lend their distinctive flavours; other common additives are crushed ice or water. It is often served as a cooling accompaniment to a curry.

cucumber, celery, apple and spinach juice

1 telegraph cucumber (400g), chopped coarsely
2 trimmed celery stalks (200g), chopped coarsely
2 large green apples (400g), cored, chopped coarsely
50g baby spinach leaves, stems removed
1 cup (250ml) water
⅓ cup firmly packed fresh mint leaves

1 Blend ingredients, in batches, until pureed;
strain through coarse sieve into large jug.

makes 1 litre (4 cups)
per 250ml 0.3g fat (0g saturated);
230kJ (55 cal); 11.9g carb
tips Refrigerate all ingredients before
making the juice.
Serve the juice within 30 minutes of making.

papaya, strawberry and orange juice

1 large papaya (1.2kg),
 chopped coarsely
250g strawberries
¾ cup (180ml) fresh
 orange juice

1 Blend papaya, strawberries
and orange juice until smooth.

makes 1 litre (4 cups)
per 250ml 0.3g fat
(0g saturated); 368kJ
(88 cal); 19.4g carb
tips Refrigerate all ingredients
before making the juice.
Serve the juice within
30 minutes of making.

orange, carrot and ginger juice

1 large orange (300g), peeled,
   chopped coarsely
1 small carrot (70g),
   halved lengthways
2cm piece fresh ginger (10g)

1 Push orange, carrot and
ginger through juice extractor.
Stir to combine.

makes 1 cup (250ml)
per 250ml 0.3g fat
(0g saturated); 439kJ
(105 cal); 22.2g carb
tips Refrigerate all ingredients
before making the juice.
Serve the juice within
30 minutes of making.

tropical delight

*You need about 400g of peeled and chopped
pineapple for this recipe.*

1 small pineapple (800g), peeled, chopped coarsely
4 medium apples (600g), chopped coarsely
2 medium oranges (480g), peeled, chopped coarsely

1 Push fruit through juice extractor. Stir to combine.

makes 1 litre (4 cups)
per 250ml 0.3g fat (0g saturated);
548kJ (131 cal); 30g carb
tips Refrigerate all ingredients before
making the juice.
Serve the juice within 30 minutes of making.

tomato, carrot and red capsicum juice

1 medium red capsicum (250g), chopped coarsely
4 medium tomatoes (300g), chopped coarsely
2 medium carrots (240g), chopped coarsely
⅓ cup firmly packed fresh flat-leaf parsley
1 cup (250ml) water
dash Tabasco sauce

1 Blend capsicum, tomato, carrot, parsley and water, in batches, until pureed; strain through coarse sieve into large jug.
2 Stir in Tabasco.

makes 1 litre (4 cups)
per 250ml 0.2g fat (0g saturated); 146kJ (35 cal); 6.1g carb
tips Refrigerate all ingredients before making the juice.
Serve the juice within 30 minutes of making.

mango and grapefruit juice

½ medium mango (215g),
   skinned, chopped coarsely
1 small grapefruit (350g),
   juiced
¼ cup (60ml) water

1 Blend ingredients
until smooth.

makes 1 cup (250ml)
per 250ml 0.8g fat
(0g saturated); 635kJ
(152 cal); 31.2g carb
tips Refrigerate all ingredients
before making the juice.
Serve the juice within
30 minutes of making.
Alternatively, for a refreshing
granita-like snack, freeze
the juice until almost frozen
then quickly mix with a fork
before drinking.

watermelon and mint juice

450g watermelon flesh,
  chopped coarsely
4 mint leaves

1 Blend ingredients
until smooth.

makes 1 cup (250ml)
per 250ml 1g fat
(0g saturated); 447kJ
(107 cal); 22.9g carb
tips Refrigerate all ingredients
before making the juice.
Serve the juice within
30 minutes of making.

beetroot, carrot and spinach juice

1 small beetroot (100g), chopped coarsely
1 small carrot (70g), chopped coarsely
1 cup firmly packed baby spinach leaves (20g)
½ cup (125ml) water

1 Push beetroot, carrot and spinach through juice extractor. Dilute with the water; stir to combine.

makes 1 cup (250ml)
per 250ml 0.2g fat (0g saturated); 230kJ
(55 cal); 10.8g carb
tips Refrigerate all ingredients before making the juice.
Serve the juice within 30 minutes of making.

fruity vegetable juice

2 medium beetroot (600g), trimmed, quartered
3 trimmed celery sticks (225g)
3 medium carrots (360g), halved lengthways
2 small apples (260g), quartered
2 medium oranges (480g), peeled, quartered

1 Push ingredients through juice extractor.
Stir to combine.

makes 1 litre (4 cups)
per 250ml 0.4g fat (0g saturated); 602kJ
(144 cal); 30.6g carb
tips Refrigerate all ingredients before making the juice.
Serve the juice within 30 minutes of making.
For a more tart drink, substitute 1 large grapefruit
(500g) for the oranges.

mixed berry smoothie

250ml frozen low-fat
  strawberry yogurt,
  softened slightly
1⅓ cups (200g) frozen
  mixed berries
3 cups (750ml) no-fat milk

1 Blend ingredients, in
batches, until smooth.
2 Serve immediately.

makes 1 litre (4 cups)
per 250ml 3.6g fat
(2.3g saturated); 803kJ
(192 cal); 27.9g carb

banana passionfruit soy smoothie

You need about six passionfruit for this recipe.

½ cup (125ml)
   passionfruit pulp
2 cups (500ml) soy milk
2 medium ripe bananas
   (400g), chopped coarsely

1 Strain passionfruit pulp through sieve into small bowl; reserve liquid and seeds.
2 Blend passionfruit liquid, milk and banana, in batches, until smooth.
3 Pour smoothie into large jug; stir in reserved seeds.

makes 1 litre (4 cups)
per 250ml 4.7g fat
(0.5g saturated); 656kJ
(157 cal); 22.5g carb

banana smoothie

2 cups (500ml) no-fat milk
2 medium bananas (400g), chopped coarsely
½ cup (140g) low-fat yogurt
1 tablespoon honey
1 tablespoon wheat germ
¼ teaspoon ground cinnamon

1 Blend ingredients until smooth.

makes 1 litre (4 cups)
per 250ml 0.9g fat (0.5g saturated); 698kJ
(167 cal); 30.5g carb

sweet saffron lassi

*Lassis are yogurt-based drinks which are an
excellent cooling foil for a fiery Indian curry.*

pinch saffron threads
1 tablespoon boiling water
2 cups (560g) yogurt
1 cup (250ml) iced water
2 tablespoons caster sugar
½ teaspoon ground cardamom
ice cubes

1 Combine saffron and the boiling water in
small heatproof cup; stand 5 minutes.
2 Whisk yogurt, the iced water, sugar and
cardamom in large jug; stir in saffron mixture.
3 Serve lassi over ice cubes.

makes 3 cups (750ml)
per 250ml 6.4g fat (4.1g saturated); 782kJ
(187 cal); 22.1g carb

coconut mango thickshake

3 medium mangoes (1.3kg)
200ml can coconut milk
1½ cups (375ml) milk
500ml vanilla ice-cream, chopped

1 Cut mango flesh from both sides of the
seed. Remove the skin and freeze mango
for several hours or until firm.
2 Blend milks, mango and ice-cream, in two
batches, until smooth. Serve immediately.

serves 6
per serving 14.1g fat (10.6g saturated); 1145kJ
(274 cal); 31.9g carb
tip For a reduced-fat version of the thickshake,
substitute light coconut milk, no-fat milk and
low-fat ice-cream. You can also use peaches,
nectarines, plums, apricots, bananas or berries,
or a combination if you prefer, instead of the mango.

pineapple orange frappé

1 medium pineapple (1.25kg),
    chopped coarsely
½ cup (125ml) orange juice
3 cups crushed ice
1 tablespoon finely grated
    orange rind

1 Blend pineapple and juice,
in batches, until smooth.
2 Pour into large jug with
crushed ice and rind; stir to
combine. Serve immediately.

makes 1 litre (4 cups)
per 250ml 0.2g fat
(0g saturated); 309kJ
(74 cal); 16g carb

mango frappé

2 medium mangoes (860g)
3 cups ice cubes
1 tablespoon sugar

1 Halve mangoes, peel, then discard seeds. Blend or process mango flesh with ice cubes and sugar until thick and smooth.
2 Pour into serving glasses; stand at room temperature for 5 minutes before serving.

makes 3 cups (750ml)
per 250ml 0.4g fat (0g saturated); 569kJ (136 cal); 31.3g carb

minted tomato, rhubarb and lime frappé

4 cups chopped rhubarb (440g)
¼ cup (55g) sugar
¼ cup (60ml) water
4 medium tomatoes (760g), peeled,
    seeded, chopped
2½ tablespoons lime juice
3 cups ice cubes
2 tablespoons chopped fresh mint

1 Combine rhubarb, sugar and the water in medium saucepan; simmer, covered, about 10 minutes or until rhubarb is tender. Cool.
2 Blend or process rhubarb mixture with remaining ingredients until smooth; serve immediately.

makes 1.25 litres (5 cups)
per 250ml 0.4g fat (0g saturated); 334kJ (80 cal); 15.4g carb

fresh berry frappé

300g blueberries
250g raspberries
4 cups crushed ice
1 cup (250ml) fresh
   orange juice

1 Blend berries until just smooth. Push berry puree through fine sieve into large bowl; discard solids in sieve.
2 Stir in ice and juice and spoon into serving glasses; serve immediately.

makes 1 litre (4 cups)
per 250ml 0.4g fat (0g saturated); 338kJ (81 cal); 17g carb
tips Depending of the sweetness of the berries, you may need to add sugar. You can crush the ice in a blender or food processor. You can also use frozen berries for this recipe. Experiment with other berries – strawberries, blackberries, boysenberries – and adjust combinations to your taste.

raspberry cranberry crush

1 cup (250ml) raspberry sorbet
2 cups (500ml) cranberry juice
1 cup (150g) frozen
   raspberries
2 tablespoons lemon juice

1 Blend or process
ingredients until smooth;
serve immediately.

makes 1 litre (4 cups)
per 250ml 0.2g fat
(0g saturated); 543kJ
(130 cal); 31.1g carb
tip Add a little icing sugar if
you prefer this drink sweeter.

iced mocha

1 tablespoon instant coffee powder
1 tablespoon boiling water
2 tablespoons chocolate-flavoured topping
1½ cups (375ml) cold milk
4 scoops (500ml) vanilla ice-cream
½ cup (125ml) cream, whipped
1 teaspoon drinking chocolate

1 Combine coffee and the water in large heatproof jug, stir until dissolved.
2 Stir in chocolate-flavoured topping and milk. Pour into two large glasses and top each with 2 scoops vanilla ice-cream and cream, then sprinkle with sifted drinking chocolate; serve immediately.

serves 2
per serving 43.9g fat (28.7g saturated); 2696kJ (645 cal); 52.7g carb

spiced iced coffee milkshake

¼ cup (20g) ground espresso coffee
¾ cup (180ml) boiling water
2 cardamom pods, bruised
¼ teaspoon ground cinnamon
1 tablespoon brown sugar
3 scoops (375ml) low-fat vanilla ice-cream
2½ cups (625ml) no-fat milk

1 Place coffee then the water in coffee plunger; stand 2 minutes before plunging. Pour coffee into small heatproof bowl with cardamom, cinnamon and sugar; stir to dissolve sugar then cool 10 minutes.
2 Strain coffee mixture through fine sieve into blender or processor; process with ice-cream and milk until smooth. Serve immediately.

makes 1 litre (4 cups)
per 250ml 3g fat (2g saturated);
640kJ (153 cal); 21.6g carb

vanilla cafe latte

⅓ cup (30g) coarsely ground
    coffee beans
500ml (2 cups) milk
1 teaspoon vanilla extract

1 Combine ingredients
in medium saucepan, stir,
over low heat until heated
through, but not boiling.
2 Pour through fine strainer
into heatproof serving glasses.

serves 2
per serving 9.9g fat
(6.5g saturated); 765kJ
(183 cal); 13.6g carb

spiced chocolate milk

30g dark eating chocolate,
  melted
2 cups (500ml) milk
1 cinnamon stick

1 Using a teaspoon, drizzle melted chocolate onto the insides of heatproof glasses.
2 Combine milk and cinnamon stick in medium saucepan, stir over low heat until heated through, but not boiling. Remove cinnamon. Pour milk into glasses.

serves 2
per serving 14.1g fat (9g saturated); 1020kJ (244 cal); 21.5g carb

real hot chocolate

1 litre (4 cups) milk
200g milk eating chocolate, chopped
100g dark eating chocolate, chopped
¾ cup (180ml) thickened cream
1 tablespoon Tia Maria or Baileys Irish Cream
90g Maltesers, chopped

1 Combine milk and both chocolates in medium saucepan; stir over low heat until chocolate is melted. Do not boil milk.
2 Beat cream and liqueur in small bowl of electric mixer until soft peaks form.
3 Divide milk among heatproof serving glasses, top with cream mixture and sprinkle with Maltesers.

serves 6
per serving 35.3g fat (24g saturated); 2328kJ (557 cal); 50.6g carb

masala chai

For this spicy traditional Indian milk tea, we used
English Breakfast tea – but try experimenting with
other varieties until you find one that suits your taste.

2 cinnamon sticks
1 teaspoon cardamom pods, bruised
1 teaspoon fennel seeds
½ teaspoon whole cloves
1 teaspoon ground ginger
½ teaspoon ground nutmeg
½ cup firmly packed fresh mint leaves
4 teabags
2 cups (500ml) milk
2 cups (500ml) water
sugar

1 Combine spices, mint and teabags in
teapot or heatproof jug. Bring combined milk
and water to a boil, pour over spice mixture;
stand 10 minutes.
2 Sweeten with a little sugar, if desired.
Just before serving, strain.

makes 1 litre (4 cups)
per 250ml 5g fat (3.2g saturated); 418kJ
(100 cal); 9.8g carb

spiced tea punch

1 litre (4 cups) water
4 teabags
1 cinnamon stick
2 cardamom pods
4 whole cloves
1 cup (220g) caster sugar
1½ cups (375ml) cold water, extra
½ cup (125ml) fresh lemon juice
2 cups (500ml) fresh orange juice
1 medium lemon (140g), sliced
¼ cup coarsely chopped fresh mint
1 litre (4 cups) mineral water
ice cubes

1 In a large saucepan, bring the water to a boil;
add teabags, spices and sugar. Stir over low heat
for about 3 minutes or until sugar is dissolved;
discard teabags. Refrigerate until cold.
2 Discard spices then stir in the extra water,
juices, lemon and mint. Just before serving,
add mineral water and ice cubes.

makes 3 litres (12 cups)
per 250ml 0.1g fat (0g saturated); 376kJ
(90 cal); 22g carb
tip The tea mixture can be made a day ahead;
store, covered, in the refrigerator.

tropical punch

You need half a medium pineapple, weighing approximately 650g, for this recipe.

425g can sliced mango in natural juice
3 cups (750ml) tropical fruit juice
300g finely chopped pineapple
250g finely chopped strawberries
2 tablespoons finely shredded fresh mint
1 tablespoon caster sugar
3 cups (750ml) dry ginger ale

1 Strain mango over small bowl; reserve juice. Chop mango slices finely; combine mango and reserved juice in large bowl with tropical fruit juice. Stir in pineapple, strawberries, mint, sugar and ginger ale.
2 Refrigerate punch 2 hours before serving.

makes 2.5 litres (10 cups)
per 250ml 0.1g fat (0g saturated); 314kJ (75 cal); 17.7g carb

tomato, apple and ginger punch

1 medium red apple (150g)
8cm piece fresh ginger (40g), grated finely
125g strawberries, quartered
2 cups (500ml) apple juice
1½ cups (375ml) tomato juice
3 cups (750ml) dry ginger ale

1 Core and chop apple. Over small bowl,
press ginger between two teaspoons to extract
juice; discard pulp. Combine apple and strawberries
in large jug, add ginger juice and remaining
juices; mix well.
2 Cover, refrigerate until cold. Just before serving,
add cold ginger ale.

makes 2 litres (8 cups)
per 250ml 0.1g fat (0g saturated); 355kJ
(85 cal); 21g carb
tip This recipe can be made a day ahead, but hold
off on adding the ginger ale until just before serving.

mixed berry punch

1 teabag
1 cup (250ml) boiling water
120g raspberries
150g blueberries
125g strawberries, halved
¼ cup loosely packed fresh mint leaves
750ml chilled sparkling apple cider
2½ cups (625ml) chilled lemonade

1 Place teabag in heatproof mug, cover with the water; stand 10 minutes. Squeeze teabag over mug, discard teabag; cool tea 10 minutes.
2 Using fork, crush raspberries in punch bowl; add blueberries, strawberries, mint and tea. Stir to combine, cover; refrigerate 1 hour. Stir cider and lemonade into punch just before serving; sprinkle with extra mint leaves, if desired.

serves 8
per serving 0.1g fat (0g saturated); 422kJ (101 cal); 18.5g carb

sparkling fruity punch

2 litres (8 cups) orange and passionfruit juice drink
850ml can unsweetened pineapple juice
250g strawberries, chopped
¼ cup (60ml) passionfruit pulp
2 medium red apples (300g), chopped
2 medium oranges (360g), peeled, chopped
1.25 litres (5 cups) lemon soda squash
1.25 litres (5 cups) creaming soda
3 cups (750ml) ginger beer
fresh mint sprigs

1 Combine orange and passionfruit juice drink, pineapple juice and fruit in large bowl.
2 Just before serving, stir in remaining ingredients. Serve cold.

makes 6.5 litres (26 cups)
per 250ml 0.2g fat (0g saturated); 326kJ (78 cal); 18.2g carb
tip Refrigerate all ingredients before making the punch. Punch base can be prepared several hours ahead; add sparkling drinks just before serving.

moroccan mint tea

1 litre (4 cups) hot water
3 teabags
1 cup loosely packed fresh
   mint leaves
2 tablespoons caster sugar
½ cup loosely packed fresh
   mint leaves, extra
1 cup ice cubes

1 Combine the water, teabags, mint and sugar in medium heatproof jug, stand 10 minutes; discard teabags. Cover; refrigerate until cool.
2 Strain tea mixture; discard leaves. Add extra mint and ice cubes; serve immediately.

makes 1 litre (4 cups)
per 250ml 0.2g fat
(0g saturated); 176kJ
(42 cal); 9.8g carb

lemon iced tea

3 teabags
3 lemon soother or
   lemon zinger teabags
1.5 litres (6 cups) boiling water
⅓ cup (80g) caster sugar
2 strips of lemon rind
1 cup ice cubes

1 Combine teabags, the water, sugar and rind in large heatproof jug, stir until sugar is dissolved; cool to room temperature, strain mixture.
2 Refrigerate until cold. Serve with ice cubes.

makes 1.5 litres (6 cups)
per 250ml 0g fat
(0g saturated); 217kJ
(52 cal); 13.4g carb

lemon grass and ginger iced tea

6 lemon grass and ginger teabags
1 litre (4 cups) boiling water
2 tablespoons grated palm sugar
10cm stick fresh lemon grass (20g), chopped finely
½ small orange (90g), sliced thinly
½ lemon, sliced thinly
¼ cup firmly packed fresh mint leaves, torn
1 cup ice cubes

1 Place teabags and the water in large heatproof jug; stand 5 minutes.
2 Discard teabags. Add sugar, lemon grass, orange and lemon to jug; stir to combine. Refrigerate, covered, until cold.
3 Stir mint into cold tea; serve immediately over ice.

makes 1 litre (4 cups)
per 250ml 0.1g fat (0g saturated); 159kJ (38 cal); 8.5g carb

lime and mint spritzer

1 cup (250ml) lime juice
1.25 litres (5 cups) chilled mineral water
¼ cup coarsely chopped fresh mint
sugar syrup
½ cup (125ml) water
½ cup (110g) caster sugar

1 Make sugar syrup.
2 Combine syrup in large jug with juice, mineral water and mint. Serve immediately, with ice if desired.
sugar syrup Combine ingredients in small saucepan; stir over heat until sugar dissolves. Bring to a boil, remove from heat; refrigerate until cold.

serves 8
per serving 0.1g fat (0g saturated); 252kJ (60 cal); 14.2g carb

homemade lemonade

4 medium lemons (560g)
4 cups (880g) caster sugar
2 cups (500ml) water
5 litres (20 cups) mineral water

1 Remove rind from lemons using a vegetable peeler, avoiding white pith; reserve lemons. Combine rind, sugar and the water in large saucepan; stir over low heat, without boiling, until sugar is dissolved. Bring to a boil, simmer, uncovered, without stirring, about 10 minutes or until syrup is thickened slightly; cool.
2 Squeeze juice from lemons – you will need 1 cup (250ml) lemon juice. Add juice to syrup, strain into jug; cover, keep refrigerated.
3 Just before serving, add four parts mineral water to one part lemonade, or to taste.

makes 6.25 litres (25 cups) diluted lemonade or 1.25 litres (5 cups) undiluted lemonade
per 250ml (diluted) 0g fat (0g saturated); 293kJ (70 cal); 17.8g carb

glossary

apple, green we used granny smith apples – crisp, juicy apples with a rich green skin.

baileys irish cream a smooth and creamy natural blend of fresh Irish cream, the finest Irish spirits, Irish whiskey, cocoa and vanilla.

beetroot also known as red beets; firm, round root vegetable.

capsicum also known as bell pepper or, simply, pepper. They can be red, green, yellow, orange or purplish black. Seeds and membranes should be discarded before use.

cardamom native to India and used extensively in its cuisine; can be purchased in pod, seed or ground form. Has a distinctive aromatic, sweetly rich flavour and is one of the world's most expensive spices.

chocolate
dark eating: made of cocoa liquor, cocoa butter and sugar.

drinking chocolate: sweetened cocoa powder.
milk: we used eating-quality milk chocolate.
flavoured topping: used to flavour drinks and as a topping for desserts such as ice-cream.

cinnamon dried inner bark of the shoots of the cinnamon tree.

clove dried flower buds of a tropical tree; can be used whole or in ground form. Have a strong scent and taste so should be used minimally.

cream
fresh: (minimum fat content 35%) also known as pure cream and pouring cream; has no additives.
thickened: (minimum fat content 35%) whipping cream containing a thickener.

creaming soda a sweet carbonated drink.

fennel dried seeds having a licorice flavour.

ginger also known as green or root ginger; the thick gnarled root of a tropical plant. Can be kept,

peeled, covered with dry sherry in a jar and refrigerated, or frozen in an airtight container.

ginger ale a ginger-flavoured carbonated drink.

ginger, ground also known as powdered ginger; used as a flavouring in cakes, pies and puddings but cannot be substituted for fresh ginger.

lemon grass a tall, clumping, lemon-smelling and tasting, sharp-edged grass; the white lower part of the stem is used, finely chopped, in cooking.

lemon soda squash a lemon flavoured carbonated drink.

maltesers chocolates with crisp, light honeycomb centres; made from chocolate, glucose syrup, malt extract, milk powder, flour and sugar.

mango tropical fruit with skin colour ranging from green through yellow to deep red. Fragrant deep yellow flesh surrounds a large flat seed.

milk, coconut not the juice found inside the fruit, which is known as coconut water, but the diluted liquid from the second pressing from the white meat of a mature coconut (the first pressing produces coconut cream). Available in cans and cartons at supermarkets.

nectar thick fruit juice.

nutmeg is available in ground form or you can grate your own with a fine grater.

papaya also known as pawpaw, it's a large, pear-shaped red-orange tropical fruit. Sometimes used unripe (green) in cooking.

parsley, flat-leaf also known as continental parsley and italian parsley.

rhubarb thick, celery-like stalked vegetable, eaten as a fruit. Only the stalk is edible; the leaves are toxic and must not be eaten.

rind also known as zest.

saffron stigma of a member of the crocus family, available in strands or ground form; imparts a yellow-orange colour to food once infused. Quality varies greatly; the best is the most expensive spice in the world. Should be stored in the freezer.

spinach correct name for this leafy green vegetable; often called english spinach or, incorrectly, silverbeet.

sugar we used coarse, granulated table sugar, also known as crystal sugar, unless otherwise specified.

brown: an extremely soft, fine granulated sugar retaining molasses for its characteristic colour and flavour.

caster: also known as superfine or finely granulated table sugar.

palm: also known as nam tan pip, jaggery, jawa or gula melaka; made from the sap of the sugar palm tree. Light brown to black in colour and usually sold in rock-hard cakes; substitute it with brown sugar if unavailable.

tabasco brand name of an extremely fiery sauce made from vinegar, hot red peppers and salt.

telegraph cucumber long and green with ridges running down its entire length; also known as continental cucumber.

tia maria coffee-flavoured liqueur.

vanilla extract obtained from vanilla beans infused in water. A non-alcoholic version of essence.

vanilla ice-cream, low-fat we used an ice-cream containing 3% fat.

watermelon large green-skinned melon with crisp, juicy red flesh.

wheat germ small creamy flakes milled from the embryo of the wheat.

yogurt, low-fat we used yogurt with a fat content of less than 0.2%.

index

facts & figures

These conversions are approximate only, but the difference between an exact and the approximate conversion of various liquid and dry measures is minimal and will not affect your cooking results.

Measuring equipment
The difference between one country's measuring cups and another's is, at most, within a 2 or 3 teaspoon variance. (For the record, 1 Australian metric measuring cup holds approximately 250ml.) The most accurate way of measuring dry ingredients is to weigh them. For liquids, use a clear glass or plastic jug having metric markings.

Note: NZ, Canada, US and UK all use 15ml tablespoons. Australian tablespoons measure 20ml. All cup and spoon measurements are level.

How to measure
When using graduated measuring cups, shake dry ingredients loosely into the appropriate cup. Do not tap the cup on a bench or tightly pack the ingredients unless directed to do so. Level the top of measuring cups and measuring spoons with a knife. When measuring liquids, place a clear glass or plastic jug having metric markings on a flat surface to check accuracy at eye level.

Dry measures

metric	imperial
15g	½oz
30g	1oz
60g	2oz
90g	3oz
125g	4oz (¼lb)
155g	5oz
185g	6oz
220g	7oz
250g	8oz (½lb)
280g	9oz
315g	10oz
345g	11oz
375g	12oz (¾lb)
410g	13oz
440g	14oz
470g	15oz
500g	16oz (1lb)
750g	24oz (1½lb)
1kg	32oz (2lb)

We use large eggs with an average weight of 60g.

Liquid measures

metric	imperial
30 ml	1 fluid oz
60 ml	2 fluid oz
100 ml	3 fluid oz
125 ml	4 fluid oz
150 ml	5 fluid oz (¼ pint/1 gill)
190 ml	6 fluid oz
250 ml (1cup)	8 fluid oz
300 ml	10 fluid oz (½ pint)
500 ml	16 fluid oz
600 ml	20 fluid oz (1 pint)
1000 ml (1litre)	1¾ pints

Helpful measures

metric	imperial
3mm	⅛in
6mm	¼in
1cm	½in
2cm	¾in
2.5cm	1in
6cm	2½in
8cm	3in
20cm	8in
23cm	9in
25cm	10in
30cm	12in (1ft)

Oven temperatures
These oven temperatures are only a guide for conventional ovens. For fan-forced ovens, check the manufacturer's manual.

	°C (Celsius)	°F (Fahrenheit)	Gas Mark
Very slow	120	250	½
Slow	150	275 – 300	1 – 2
Moderately slow	160	325	3
Moderate	180	350 – 375	4 – 5
Moderately hot	200	400	6
Hot	220	425 – 450	7 – 8
Very hot	240	475	9

ARE YOU MISSING SOME OF THE WORLD'S FAVOURITE COOKBOOKS?

The Australian Women's Weekly cookbooks are available from bookshops, cookshops, supermarkets and other stores all over the world. You can also buy direct from the publisher, using the order form below.

Mini Series £2.50 190x138mm 64 pages			
	QTY		QTY
4 Fast Ingredients		Italian	
15-minute Feasts		Jams & Jellies	
30-minute Meals		Kids Party Food	
50 Fast Chicken Fillets		Last-minute Meals	
After-work Stir-fries		Lebanese Cooking	
Barbecue		Malaysian Favourites	
Barbecue Chicken		Microwave	
Barbecued Seafood		Mince	
Biscuits, Brownies & Biscotti		Muffins	
Bites		Noodles	
Bowl Food		Party Food	
Burgers, Rösti & Fritters		Pasta	
Cafe Cakes		Pickles and Chutneys	
Cafe Food		Potatoes	
Casseroles		Risotto	
Char-grills & Barbecues		Roast	
Cheesecakes, Pavlovas & Trifles		Salads	
Chocolate		Seafood	
Chocolate Cakes		Simple Slices	
Christmas Cakes & Puddings		Simply Seafood	
Cocktails		Skinny Food	
Curries		Stir-fries	
Drinks		Summer Salads	
Fast Fish		Tapas, Antipasto & Mezze	
Fast Food for Friends		Thai Cooking	
Fast Soup		Thai Favourites	
Finger Food		Vegetarian	
From the Shelf		Vegetarian Stir-fries	
Gluten-free Cooking		Vegie Main Meals	
Ice-creams & Sorbets		Wok	
Indian Cooking		**TOTAL COST**	**£**

NAME

ADDRESS

POSTCODE

DAYTIME PHONE

I ENCLOSE MY CHEQUE/MONEY ORDER FOR £

OR PLEASE CHARGE MY VISA, ACCESS OR MASTERCARD NUMBER

CARDHOLDER'S NAME

EXPIRY DATE

CARDHOLDER'S SIGNATURE

To order: Mail or fax – photocopy or complete the order form above, and send your credit card details or cheque payable to: Australian Consolidated Press (UK), Moulton Park Business Centre, Red House Road, Moulton Park, Northampton NN3 6AQ, phone (+44) (01) 604 497531, fax (+44) (01) 604 497533, e-mail books@acpuk.com. Or order online at **www.acpuk.com**

Non-UK residents: We accept the credit cards listed on the coupon, or cheques, drafts or International Money Orders payable in sterling and drawn on a UK bank. Credit card charges are at the exchange rate current at the time of payment.

Postage and packing UK: Add £1.00 per order plus 25p per book.
Postage and packing overseas: Add £2.00 per order plus 50p per book.
Offer ends 31.12.2006

Food director Pamela Clark
Food editor Louise Patniotis
Nutritional information Angela Muscat
ACP BOOKS
Editorial director Susan Tomnay
Creative director Hieu Chi Nguyen
Senior editor Julie Collard
Designer Josii Do
Sales director Brian Cearnes
Brand manager Renée Crea
Production manager Carol Currie
Chief executive officer John Alexander
Group publisher Pat Ingram
Publisher Sue Wannan
Editorial director (AWW) Deborah Thomas

Produced by ACP Books, Sydney.
Printing by Times Printers, Singapore.
Published by ACP Publishing Pty Limited,
54 Park St, Sydney;
GPO Box 4088, Sydney, NSW 2001.
Ph: (02) 9282 8618 Fax: (02) 9267 9438.
acpbooks@acp.com.au
www.acpbooks.com.au
To order books phone 136 116.
Send recipe enquiries to
Recipeenquiries@acp.com.au
RIGHTS ENQUIRIES
Laura Bamford, Director ACP Books.
lbamford@acplon.co.uk
Ph: +44 (207) 812 6526
Australia Distributed by Network Services,
GPO Box 4088, Sydney, NSW 1028.
Ph: (02) 9282 8777 Fax: (02) 9264 3278.
United Kingdom Distributed by Australian
Consolidated Press (UK), Moulton Park Busi
Centre, Red House Road, Moulton Park,
Northampton, NN3 6AQ. Ph: (01604) 497 5
Fax: (01604) 497 533 acpukltd@aol.com
Canada Distributed by Whitecap Books Ltd,
351 Lynn Ave, North Vancouver, BC, V7J 2C
Ph: (604) 980 9852 Fax: (604) 980 8197
customerservice@whitecap.ca
www.whitecap.ca
New Zealand Distributed by Netlink Distribu
Company, ACP Media Centre, Cnr Fanshaw
and Beaumont Streets, Westhaven, Aucklan
PO Box 47906, Ponsonby, Auckland, NZ.
Ph: (9) 366 9966 ask@ndcnz.co.nz
South Africa Distributed by PSD Promotions
30 Diesel Road, Isando, Gauteng, Johannes
PO Box 1175, Isando, 1600, Gauteng, Johan
Ph: (27 11) 392 6065/6/7 Fax: (27 11) 392 6
orders@psdprom.co.za

Clark, Pamela.
The Australian Women's Weekly
Drinks

Includes index.
ISBN 1 86396 424 X

1. Non-alcoholic beverages.
2. Smoothies (beverages). I. Title.
II. Title: Australian Women's Weekly.

641.875

© ACP Publishing Pty Limited 2005
ABN 18 053 273 546

Cover Fruity vegetable juice, page 16.
Stylist Kate Brown
Photographer Tanya Zouev
Home economist Kirrily Smith
Back cover at left, Raspberry cranberry cru
page 31; at right, Homemade lemonade, pa